Old BEITH

by
Donald L. Reid

A view of Beith from Kerse Road at the turn of the twentieth century. At that time Beith Cemetery in the foreground was an open grass area whereas today it is full of gravestones. Behind it is the cabinet works of Stevenson, Higgins and Company which was formed in 1886 at Janefield. The dominant tower was built together with an extension to the factory in 1901 and a showroom was added in 1927. Janefield, renowned for making lift cabinets, finally closed its doors for the last time in 1965.

This book is respectfully dedicated to the memory of Dr John Hibberd, 1945–2000, a Gateside resident, Chairman of the Gateside Village Hall Committee and a popular and respected general practitioner in Beith and district from 1973 until his death in March, 2000.
"The social, friendly, honest man,/ Whate'er he be,/ Tis he fulfils great Nature's plan,/ And none but he."   Robert Burns, 'Second Epistle to J. Lapraik'

Auld Kirk
Beith

© Donald L. Reid, 2000
First published in the United Kingdom, 2000,
by Stenlake Publishing, Ochiltree Sawmill, The Lade,
Ochiltree, Ayrshire, KA18 2NX
Telephone / Fax: 01290 423114

ISBN 1 84033 126 7

The author's fee for writing this book has been donated to the Duke of
Edinburgh's Award at Beith (North Ayrshire) Open Award Group.

ACKNOWLEDGEMENTS

I am indebted to the following individuals for their kind assistance in the
compilation of this book: George Anderson, Robert Boyd, Tom Boyd, Dillie
Etherington, Jessie Fairns, William Fairns, Dr Arthur Jamieson, Sheila Jamieson,
Adam Johnstone, Franciso Haro of Stewarton, John Irvine, J.R. 'Ian' Kerr, Tom
'T.J.' McAllister, Katherine McGregor, David McMillan, William McMillan,
Irene MacPherson, Isobel Monahan, Angela Mackie, Sandy Mackie, James
Muir of Barrmill, Catherine McMaster, Harry McMaster J.P., Janet Osborne,
Jimmy Quinn, Kathleen Reid, Alex Sanderson, Iain Shaw of Houston, John
Boyd Smith, Billy Steel and Hugh Waterston.
    The pictures on pages 7, 9, 21, 22–25, 27, 29, 31, 38–40, 42–44 and the inside
back cover are reproduced courtesy of North Ayrshire Libraries. The publishers
wish to thank Jill McCall of the Library Headquarters in Ardrossan for her help.

The Auld Kirk is a permanent reminder of the Beith of yesteryear. The rather
insensitive road systems developed in the early 1970s tore the heart out of the
old town and, in the view of many local people, damaged its integrity, isolating
the old church between the workaday town and the charms of Eglinton Street.
The old bell, still in position today, bears the following inscription: *This bell
was given by Hew Montgomerie son to Hesilhead anno 1614 and refounded by the
heritors of Beith anno 1734. R.M. & Company Fecit.* The bell was refurbished in
1999 by Robert Marshall, blacksmith of Gateside Village, and was replaced by
Smith Brothers, builders, in time to be rung by Robert Boyd, chairman of Beith
and District Community Council, at midnight on 31 December, 1999, to usher
in the Millennium.

INTRODUCTION

The Parish of Beith covers twenty-five square miles on the northern tip of Ayrshire with the town itself only one mile from the Renfrewshire border. The Parish includes Longbar, Barrmill, Burnhouse, Greenhills, Gateside and a myriad of farms and cottages in a fertile rural district famous for the excellence of its dairy products. The town of Beith is situated on the crest of a hill, known originally as the 'Hill o' Beith' or hill of the birches (the name evolved from the Gaelic word meaning birch). Further evidence that at one time much of the area was covered by forest is in other local place names such as Roughwood, Fulwoodhead, Threepwood and Woodside.

The recorded history of Beith can be traced to the sixth century when men of the Kingdom of Strathclyde waged a continual, but losing, battle "in the woods of Beith" against invading Saxons, Scots and Northmen. In the eleventh century, Beith was granted to a knight by the name of Hugh de Morville, from Cumbernauld, whose wife Avicia de Lancaster in turn granted the lands of Beith to the monastery of Kilwinning. Although the monk's land lay largely along the route of the Roebank Burn it is said that they built the first 'Mill o' Beith' with their home farm at nearby Grangehill. These monks built the first chapel for the people of Beith, still to be seen today at the Cross. The first houses of the town were clustered round the chapel and this evolved into the present town.

In 1733 forty or fifty Beith smugglers sacked the Irvine Customs House, escaping with a rich booty of confiscated contraband goods. Twelve years later many of these same men joined with the famous Rev. John Witherspoon, Minister of Beith between 1745 and 1757, when he led the men of Beith to Glasgow to defend King George III against the Young Pretender in the 1745 rebellion. Despite receiving orders to return to Beith, Witherspoon carried on and was captured at the Battle of Falkirk and imprisoned for a time in Doune Castle. After his release he later emigrated to America and became President of Princeton College and a representative in Congress of the Province of New Jersey. During the War of Independence he supported the Americans and signed the Declaration of Independence. Witherspoon's Beith home at No.32, The Cross, is now the focus for a multimillion pound regeneration which will begin in 2001.

Smuggling in Beith continued to be a problem for the authorities throughout the later 1700s and in 1789 a company of seventy-six soldiers were quartered in the town to combat illicit trade in tea, tobacco, and spirits. This caused great inconvenience to the law-abiding citizens with whom the soldiers were billeted, but the town was policed in this fashion for some time thereafter.

From a population of 2,064 in 1755, the parish grew rapidly to 2,872 in 1792, 3,103 in 1801, 3,755 in 1811 and by 1831 the figure was 5,052. By the early 1790s Beith was thriving and numerous tradespeople were required to meet the needs of the semi-rural population and many were employed in manufacturing goods for nearby Paisley and Glasgow. Beith was able to boast five lint mills, four corn mills, three licensed distillers, two candle works, a malt work, a tan-work and a tobacco manufacturing company. Seventy people were weaving muslin, sixty-three making thread, fifty spinning cotton, forty-four weaving gauze, and many females were employed in sewing and tambouring muslin embroidery. In addition there were twenty-nine shoemakers, twenty-two masons, twenty-one house-carpenters, fifteen smiths, thirteen tailors and numerous butchers, coal-hewers, flax-dressers, bakers, coopers, stocking-makers, barbers, saddlers, grocers, cloth merchants and one watchmaker. There was also a bookseller whose shop contained about 3,000 volumes.

By the turn of the nineteenth century flax dressing and handloom weaving were being superseded by the power-loom, and tanning and currying hides became important with William Barr of the Bathwell Tanning and Currying Works, and William Muir of the Bath Lane Tannery, being two shrewd businessmen and local benefactors who exploited these changes in local industry.

Cabinet and chair making would also boom in the nineteenth century. At first this was regarded as work for independent artisans who made high-class furniture from local wood in their own workshops at home. However, this workshop industry was rapidly subsumed by the modern factory system with a strict division of labour from 1860 onwards (the main positions were as labourers, sawmen, machinemen, carvers, cabinet makers, polishers, and packers). Beith names which became world famous included Matthew Pollock (owner of the Caledonia Works), John Pollock (Victoria Cabinet Works), Robert Balfour (Bark Mill and West of Scotland Cabinet Works), and Hugh Stevenson, William Stevenson and Hugh Higgins (Stevenson & Higgins of Janefield Cabinet Works). Factories were built employing hundreds of workmen and the fame of Beith furniture spread until 'Beith quality' became the standard of excellence in material, manufacture and finish. Markets served included the rest of Scotland and Great Britain, and orders came in from Spain, South Africa, Australia, New Zealand, and even South America. Sadly, the cabinet works had all closed by the early 1980s, but local people are proud of *Beith which licks creation in making chairs and tanning hides*.

Today Beith is a dormitory town with a reputation as a friendly and welcoming place in which to work, live and socialise. In 1966 a survey estimated that 48% of the population worked outside the town, while today the figure is more likely to be around 66%. The population is around 7,000, helped by the completion of ten private housing estates dating from 1966 to the present and by redevelopment of sites within the town. By 1998 around two-thirds of households in Beith had one or more cars compared to about 40% in 1966. The result is much more traffic with commensurate parking problems. The town has an abundance of social organisations for everyone and there are excellent transport links to Glasgow.

Beith from Lochfaulds

The view of Beith from the rural area of Lochfaulds to the east of the town. In the centre is Beith High Church, construction of which began in 1807 and was completed in 1810. The tower bell rang for the first time in 1811 and the poet Andrew Aitken of Overton (1779–1850), wrote the following lines commemorating this occasion: *Tis from the bell suspended in the tower/ O'erlooking Beith, to mark each passing hour/ Of time's swift progress, and, with varied sounds,/ A monitor to all the neighbouring towns.* Immediately to the left of the church is Beith Academy and the schoolmaster's house, both of which were built in 1840. The first schoolmaster was James Reid and his salary was £70 a year! This picture was taken before Mains Road and Blackthorn Avenue housing schemes were built. The chimney on the right is that of the Beith Chocolate Works which produced Valencia chocolate in both boxed and slab form. This factory was located where the tennis courts are now near Mid Road. It employed around fifteen young women and a few men and ceased operation around 1928. The derelict building was finally destroyed by fire around ten years later.

Whang Meadows & Tanyards, Beith.

The chimney in the centre indicates the location of the former Bathwell Tanning and Currying works of William Barr and the Bath Lane Tannery of William Muir. To the left of the tanyard was the old Beith gas works. Macneil's cabinet works was also established on the tanyard site in 1910, having previously been located in Dalry. However, Macneil's closed in December, 1953. The grass area on the left now incorporates Bellsdale Park which was opened in 1922 and is now the home of Beith Juniors Football Club. The high building in the centre of the picture is the rear of what is currently Beith Post Office. This building along with others at the Cross will be the subject of renovation beginning in 2001.

Main St Beith

Main Street looking south with the corner of Reform Street junction just visible on the right between the children and the man with the dog. The distinctive lantern hanging above the Masonic Arms Public House dates this photograph to the early 1900s as it was moved to the newly opened Masonic Lodge at the Cross in 1907. Meetings of Beith St John's No.157 were occasionally held in the large room above the public house. This lodge is of ancient lineage, having been formed under charter from Kilwinning on 26 December, 1754, as Beith St John's No.10. The building on the right beside the man and dog was the original home of the popular *Western Supplement* newspaper, founded in 1865, which later became *The Beith Supplement* until incorporated in the *Ardrossan & Saltcoats Herald* in 1965. *The Supplement* found its way to Beithites all over the world, keeping them in touch with news of the town and district. Even today older folk in Beith speak fondly of *The Supplement* which was read in more than half the homes in the town and district. Beyond the man and dog the men are standing outside the Victoria Tavern, owned by Mr Kydd, which was demolished in the late 1940s.

MAIN STREET, BEITH

D 5129

Main Street, 1960, again looking south towards Reform Street, with William Young standing outside his butcher's shop. William McConnell & Son, florist, is still going strong today as is the Smugglers Tavern with the prominent chimney on the right. Speeding vehicles have always been a problem on this street, even in the nineteenth century. In June 1865, *The Western Supplement* complained in its columns about the number of horses being ridden recklessly through the town "endangering the limbs and lives of young and old".

A view of Main Street taken from the Horseshoe where the older men of the town would gather to discuss the local issues of the day. The shop of Gavin Gibson, butcher, is on the left and next door was the popular baker shop of Mr Ferguson. Even in the days before cars, horse-drawn carts passing through the Main Street could cause congestion. Runaway horses were an occasional problem reported in the columns of *The Beith Supplement*. By the 1960s buses or lorries endeavouring to pass each other in the street became a nightmare for pedestrians and minor road accidents were a frequent occurrence.

The Horseshoe was the junction formed by Main Street, Wilson Street, Mitchell Street and Kings Road and was so called because its shape resembled a horseshoe. The building on the left was occupied for many years by Andrew Guy, painter. The imposing building in the centre was occupied by Hendry the grocer and on the right is the Star Hotel which was an old coaching house, later appropriately renamed the Coach House Inn. The Coach House lay derelict from April 1991 and was demolished in 1998 leaving a gap site in the town centre which has still not been filled. The last owner was Jack Fordyce.

Main Street contains a fine crop of early nineteenth century buildings. This view gives a sense of the narrowness of Main Street and clearly shows the lack of pavements which was an ongoing concern from very early times; even today there are no pavements, although the traffic now flows 'one way.' The boys are standing outside the Smugglers Tavern which was built around 1750 and is a reminder of the days between 1730 and the 1790s when Beith was infamous as a town where smugglers traded illicit goods landed on the Ayrshire coast. It made a convenient stopping-off point on the way to Paisley and Glasgow. The shop on the left was owned by R.B. Smith and sold Eagle cycles, examples of which are just visible in the shop window.

Beith Cross and the enchanting Auld Kirk which has long been the focal point of the town and of particular interest to visitors. It was built in 1593 when the minister was Rev. Johne Young. However, its history goes as far back as the ninth century and it is believed that St Inan came to Beith in 839 A.D. and preached on the Bigholm Hills above the town. Interestingly, the Cross is not so called because of the Auld Kirk, but because at one time a ford was located there to cross the Dukes Burn. The buildings on the right were all demolished in the period between 1969 and 1972 when major changes were imposed on the old town centre in connection with road realignment and development to ease congestion in the town. The restaurant on the right was formerly owned by Mr & Mrs William Hamilton who advertised in *The Western Supplement* in 1889. Mrs Hamilton's death was reported in the *Supplement* in May, 1890. By the time of this photograph the restaurant was owned by J. Gilchrist whose name can just be seen over the door.

The style and spirit of the old town centre in the days before cars is nicely captured in this photograph. The gentlemen is standing outside Gemmell the chemist. On the left is the wall of the Auld Kirk while the Main Street joins the Cross in the centre of the picture at what was a sharp left-hand bend into Main Street. The shop with the sun shades was Mortimer's Garage, later Walker's Garage until 1945 when it became The Cross Garage owned by John McLean before its closure in 1960. To its immediate left was Pieroni's fish and chip shop. Many older Beithites will recall Mary and her sons, Toni and Quinto. This shop was subjected to occasional vandalism during the Second World War simply because the family were of Italian extraction. Abutting on to the cemetery wall and out of sight was the offices of James Miller & Co., publisher and printers of *The Beith Supplement*. Older Beithites will instantly recall Shearer the barber, Wilson the butcher and Cummings the saddler as well as having fond memories of Willie Doctor's and the Beith Clothing Company.

A view of Eglinton Street, taken from the Foley (the piece of ground surrounded by a high wall between New Street and the Cross) looking south along the roughly made road. This scene is largely unchanged today with the exception of the roof now removed from the derelict Daly's grocer shop. It was a common site for horses to drink from the trough at the fountain at the foot of the Strand. The house above John Daly's grocer shop was the home of Rev. John Witherspoon, Minister of Beith (1745–1757) who signed the American Declaration of Independence and led a band of Beith men intent on taking part in the 1745 rebellion. His old home and other buildings around the Cross area will be refurbished in 2001. The Masonic Hall was built on the gap site on the bottom left corner in 1907.

Eglinton Street is the chief glory of Beith with a long gently curving run of two-storey houses on both sides. Between Crawford's the grocer and the Saracen Head Inn is the pend leading to the rear of the hotel. Two old ladies, the Miss Roys, lived above Crawford's and died in their home in a fire in the early 1950s. Through the pend was to be found a popular quoiting ground and stabling for horses. No lamp standards are to be seen on the street which is rather strange as the town had limited gas lighting from 1831, although this was probably used for domestic purposes. The Beith Gas Light Company built a large gasometer in the town on Kings Road in 1908. Lemonade was manufactured in a small factory approximately halfway along Eglinton Street on the right. It burned down in the 1920s and never reopened. There was also an aerated water factory established at Bellscauseway on the Barrmill Road by Thomas Murray in April 1891.

The Strand, Beith.

This view of the Strand looking towards Townhead is unchanged today. The building on the right was formerly the Unionist Rooms, later to become the town library on the upper floor with the health centre on the ground floor. The building is now owned and occupied by the long established builder's firm of Smith Brothers. The shop on the left with the lady in the white apron and with the man leaning on the window was the premises of William and Sarah-Louisa Howie, grocers, the great-grandparents of Ellen Hart J.P. of Beith. Advertisements for Howie's shop are to be found in *The Western Supplement* of January 1908.

Mains Road looking west with the junction of Park Avenue on the right. Mains Road was named after Mains Farm which was located towards Lochfaulds, but is no longer standing. This photograph was taken in early 1940, a few years after this housing development was built.

Reform Street, Beith.

Reform Street looking east towards Main Street. The cottage on the left and the tenement next door still stand, but all the properties on the right have been replaced mainly by council housing. Beith Health Centre is located near the top of Reform Street and was built in 1974. This street was formerly known as 'Bunswynd', a name which appears on the 1897 map of Beith. In the late nineteenth century there was a model lodging house in Bunswynd and several of the residents regularly appeared at Beith District Court for minor offences, especially drunkenness. In 1890 *The Western Supplement* reported that Beith had fifteen public houses, three hotels and ten grocers with certificates to sell alcohol, indicating that drink was readily available from a wide range of sources.

Wilson Street (formerly know as Newton Street), looking north from the Horseshoe with Hamilfield (now Trinity) Church dominating the skyline. The shop in the right foreground belonged to John Hendry, grocer, and is no longer standing, and John Telfer's is also now a gap site. There were a number of carriers or carters in the town using horse-drawn carts, so there was a lot of business for saddlers and blacksmiths. Halfway along Wilson Street was the town's last remaining thatched house which was still in existence in the early 1900s. It is an interesting coincidence that the house was the home of John Broadley, the last man in Beith to regularly follow the trade of thatcher. He and his wife Nancy were natives of Erin and were said to have been "a quaint and interesting couple".

Wardrop Street looking east towards Gateside village, prior to 1907. In the 1920s the houses on both sides of the road were replaced by the first council houses in Beith. The tenements on the right was at one time occupied by home-based loom weavers and they were known locally as the Weaver's Cottages. There were cellars below the houses where they plied their trade. By 1820 handloom weaving, once the principal occupation of Beithites, was beginning to decline markedly, but even by the late 1890s there were still a few skilled handloom weavers in the town.

Wardrop Street, Beith.

Grahamfield Place looking east towards Dalry Road. The tenements on the left are largely unchanged today. The tall building on the right was Winton Place which was occupied by railway workers as it was adjacent to Beith Town Station. Private single storey housing now occupies this site. Grahamfield Place led to Balfour's West of Scotland Furniture Works and the street was particularly busy with traffic during the rush hour in the morning and evening.

Head Street looking east at its junction on the left with New Street. The pend on the right led to the rear of Gibby Woods' Head Street Dairy. The dominant house to the left is exactly the same today except that the railings were removed in 1944 for scrap metal in support of the war effort. The little shop with writing in the window was latterly Mrs Buchanan's sweetie shop. The building with the highest chimneys was the Liberal Club and most older Beithites recall that the entrance hallway was a fine example of a 'walley close' tiled in a most handsome style. The High Level public house is shown on the left and it closed around 1963 when the last proprietor was Harry Allen. It was demolished shortly afterwards. The horse is likely to have belonged to Woods, who kept his horses in the field behind the dairy shown on the right of the picture.

This view shows Janefield Place, looking east from Kings Road. The tenement on the right was always simply known as the 'Co-op Building' and was built on ground belonging to Stevenson, Higgins & Company. Its accommodation was rented out to local people. *The Western Supplement* of 25 January, 1890 reported that "the tenement is of a substantial nature and is expected to realise a good divvy [dividend] to members . . . [the building cost] a total of £1,701 for the entire contract." The small cottage in the centre has an interesting 'figure stone' frontage and has always been known by locals as Dummy Cottage. Kings Road led to the Low Station about one mile east of this location. This station opened with the construction of the Glasgow–Ayr line in 1840. Until the opening of Beith Town Station in 1878, everyone from Beith had to either walk or travel by horse charabanc to the Low Station which was located about one and a half miles from the town centre. The scene is virtually the same today, except that Beith War Memorial is located on the right of the picture, having been re-sited from Bigholm in 1947.

Beith Station Rd.

Looking east from Beith Low Station (or Kerse) Road to Beith with the High Kirk on the right background and Stevenson & Higgin's cabinet works in the centre. The entrance to Woodside Estate is seen on the left. The road to Beith Low Station was busy with horse charabanc and carts bringing people and goods to the town and there were several firms of carters in Beith, two of the prominent ones being Gray and Woods. The building across from the Low Station was called the Railway Inn and it closed in 1949 when it reverted to a dwelling house. Beith Low Station closed in 1964.

King's Road with the High Kirk known as the 'Visible Church' because it can be seen from every approach to Beith. It is a Gothic T-plan kirk with a tall five-stage tower. The houses on both sides of the road are still standing today and Beith Community Centre has been constructed on the gap in front of the High Church. The shed on the right behind the lamp standard belonged to Tom Gray, a well-known carter who had horses and charabancs as well as carts to transport the public and goods about the town and to and from the Low and Town stations. King's Road, formerly known as New Road, was named after William King J.P. of Hillside, for many years agent for the town's branch of the Commercial Bank of Scotland. One of the positive achievements which he brought about was the tidying up of the burial ground of the Auld Kirk, in which he was later buried.

During the late 1960s several older buildings in Kings Road were demolished. This particular photograph was taken in 1975 by Hugh Waterston of Beith, a keen amateur photographer, and shows the demolition of houses at 18–24 Kings Road, adjacent to Beith Telephone Exchange. Beith Police Station, built in 1981 and currently under threat of closure, now stands on this site. This photograph was awarded a prize at the Glasgow District Photographic Union show in 1976.

Caledonia. F.C. Beith.

The first recorded game of Association Football in Beith took place on Saturday 15th May, 1875, when the Beith club played the Ladeside club of Kilbirnie in a field at Gateside Toll. Beith triumphed by one goal to nil. In these early years between 1875 and 1900, several teams were prominent in Beith. As well as Caledonia F.C. there was Beith Burnside, Beith Thistle, Beith Victoria, Beith Woodside, Roebank Rangers and Beith Athletic. Some of these teams only lasted for a short period of time before amalgamating or becoming defunct. In addition, the enthusiasm for the game had spread to the surrounding villages and about this period Gateside, Barrmill and Barkip all had teams. It is likely that Caledonia F.C. were the works team of Matthew Pollock's Caledonia Works which began operations in 1879, although he had been in business with his brother John twenty-eight years before. Beith Juniors, formed in 1938, is the local team in Beith today and they play at Bellsdale Park.

This particular photograph is intriguingly captioned simply as 'Beith Summer Visitors.' Beith, Lochwinnoch and Gateside were popular resorts for visitors from Paisley and Glasgow and such visits are well documented in the columns of *The Ardrossan & Saltcoats Herald* and *The Western Supplement* from 1865 onwards. However, this group are almost certainly not on an excursion. Their fine dress implies that they are more likely to have been attending a formal function such as a dinner or perhaps a Masonic installation. Another suggestion is that they may have been involved in a bowling tournament as bowlers of the early days were expected to dress to a standard befitting the gentlemen of the day, there being few ordinary working men in local clubs. Beith Bowling Club was established in 1865. Local enquiry has failed to reveal any further information. Perhaps readers can help to clarify the story behind this picture.

Little is known about this scene in which Beithites have donned a variety of military and civilian dress for Belgium Flag Day. It is likely that this occasion was held during the First World War to raise funds to support the war effort in Belgium. Local newspaper reports record similar events during this period such as French Red Cross Flag Day. Many clubs and organisations of the late nineteenth and early twentieth century would enjoy such fancy dress outings to the grand houses of the town and district such as Woodside, Morrishill, Trearne and Grangehill.

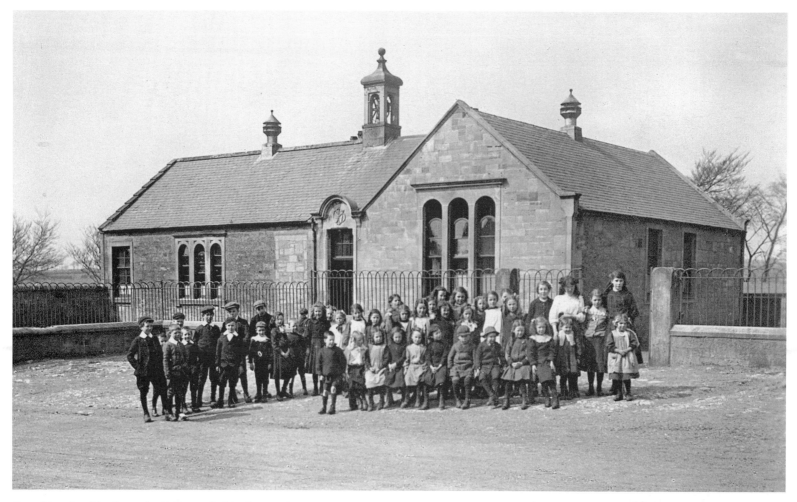

Gateside school in the early 1900s, probably during the time when Mr John Bone was headmaster. The school itself has changed little from the front, although an extension has been added to the rear. Mr Bone used to ring the distinctive bell located on the centre of the roof for every period, whereas his successor, Mr Robert Gray, insisted on using a handbell. The rope bell can still be rung today. The school is very much part of the community of Gateside and it is the venue of the annual Gateside Horticultural Society Show. The current head teacher is Mrs Agnes McGuigan and the school roll stands at fifty-six pupils.

This school on Barrmill Road, an annexe of Beith Academy, was completed in 1930 and finally demolished in 1997 to make room for a magnificent new primary school for the town. This new school was completed in 1999 and officially opened in June, 2000. All departments, including a nursery, are housed under one roof. The headteacher is Mr Tom Mabon and the current school roll is 650.

Built in 1887, Spier's School was a splendid building designed by James Sellars and set in wooded grounds on the outskirts of Beith. It was constructed of Ballochmyle stone which was brought to Barrmill by rail and then sent to Beith by horse cart. The school had a tower, hall, boardroom, ten classrooms and a schoolhouse. It was erected as a memorial to John Spier, son of Robert Spier, writer, of Marshalland and Cuff Estates, by his mother Margaret Spier and officially opened in September, 1888. It had 140 pupils, most of them from North Ayrshire, although two had followed Mr R. Bruce-Lockhart, the first headmaster, from his previous school, Waid Academy. The boys were taught separately from the girls until 1893. By 1968 Spier's had a roll of 347, but the building was beginning to deteriorate. A decision was taken to build a purpose-built secondary school for Beith, Kilbirnie and Dalry at Kilbirnie and when Garnock Academy opened in 1972, Spier's School closed and was finally demolished in 1984.

Staff and pupils of Spier's School, session 1922/23, photographed outside the school. The man in the centre is almost certainly the principal modern languages teacher, J.E.G. Burgoyne. From its inception in 1887 until its ultimate closure in June 1972, the school was regarded with great affection by pupils and staff alike and twenty-eight years after its closure you will still hear ex-pupils speak about it in almost reverential tones. The school could boast its own Scout Troop and Guide Company, and during the First World War a Boys Military Training Corps was formed. Spier's was also renowned for having excellent rugby, netball and cricket teams. During its entire existence it only had six headmasters: R. Bruce-Lockhart (1888–1895), Dr J.A. Third (1895–1919), Alexander Emslie (1919–1921), Gilbert R. Mair (1921–1937), Robert R. Fairley (1937–1963), and David K. Conn (1963–1972).

PARISH CHURCH, BEITH

B 9127

Beith High Church at the end of Kirk Road, viewed from Barrmill Road. The tenements on the left were demolished in 1960 and a bungalow now stands on the site. The large wall on the right is the boundary line of the garden of Knockbuckle House. This church was built on the hill of Knockbuckle, at the back of and overlooking the town in March, 1807. The ceremony of laying the foundation stone was heralded by a band and a procession of freemasons from various lodges. It was opened for divine service on 19 August, 1810. The square tower rises from the back of the church to a height of ninety-two feet and can be seen from any approach to Beith – consequently the building has been dubbed the 'Visible Church'. The church has seating for 1,250 people. The bell was a gift of Robert Shedden of Gower Street, London, a native of the parish and a descendent of the Sheddens of Roughwood.

This photograph probably dates from around 1890 as no older Beithite of the town or farming community can recall actually seeing Lochs Farm. All that remains today is extensive ruins on the left side of the Threepwood Road above Kirkleegreen Reservoir. Beith received gravitational water from Kirkleegreen Reservoir in 1890 and the new dam was formally opened on 12 May, 1891. It is said that this farm was demolished to prevent contamination of the water by the farm's animals. The east side of the reservoir is now lined by trees along its entire length.

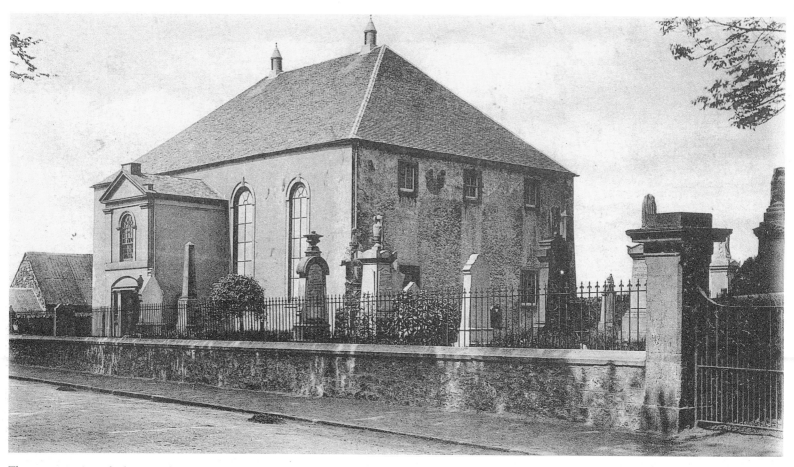

The congregation of what was the Relief church (later to become the United Presbyterian and then the United Free) was formed in this building in Head Street in 1784, their church having been built in 1783. The last minister of the congregation was Rev. John Lennox who was there from 1884 until the closure of the church in 1917. In 1916 the congregation had amalgamated with those of the Mitchell Street and Hamilfield churches and initially they met in the Head Street building as the magnificent Hamilfield church had been gutted by fire in November that year. The rebuilt church on the Hamilfield site was renamed Trinity Church because of the union of the three congregations. In the years following the closure of Head Street church the building was used in turn as the Orange Hall, the Embassy Cinema, and since 1969 the headquarters of Beith Boys Brigade. Soldiers were billeted in the hall during the Second World War. In 1953 all pupils and staff at Beith Primary School were taken to the Embassy Cinema to see footage of the coronation of Queen Elizabeth II and the conquest of Everest.

Hessilhead Castle was located about one and a half miles east of Gateside Village. It was famous as being the birthplace of the poet Alexander Montgomery (*c*.1545–1597), the laureate ('maister poete') of the Edinburgh court of James VI. Montgomerie belonged to a branch of Ayrshire's powerful Eglintoun family and his Catholicism, first employed by James in secret dealings with Philip of Spain, led finally to his exile from Scotland. His best known poems include 'The Cherry and the Slae' and his address, *To my aul maister and his young disciple, Twa bairns of Beith by nature taught and tipple*. This elegant muse sings the praise of Lady Margaret Montgomerie, eldest daughter of Hugh, third Earl of Eglintoun. In 1680 Francis Montgomerie of Giffen acquired the castle and built an addition on to the square tower on the east side to improve its accommodation. However, by 1776 the castle was falling into disrepair and Michael Carmichael, the then proprietor, unroofed it and removed part of the walls and sold the materials. In the early 1900s this was a popular destination for trips from Beith and there was still considerable ivy-clad ruins to be found. These ruins were later removed for building material and all that remain are some of the finest trees in the parish, planted by Francis Montgomerie between 1680 and the early 1700s.

Giffen House
from the garden

Built in 1869, Giffen House lies in the Parish of Dalry and was built for Henry Gardiner Patrick to the designs of Andrew Heiton Jnr. It is sited over 2 miles westward of the site of the old Castle of Giffen. Giffen House is a striking exercise in High-Victorian Scottish Baronial and is one of the few such major houses in Ayrshire to remain unaltered. The stables, built in a U-plan, are located a distance from and are contemporary with the house. In 1984 they were converted into a residence to the designs of Alan Grant for Barrmill Developments.

Morrishill House was marked as a mansion on a map of 1827, but the estate has a much older history and part of it was supposed to date from 1637. In 1737 the then owner, a William Adam, was advised to sell part of the property to escape from financial difficulties resulting from his heavy drinking; however, he objected, declaring that he would be "aye a Morishill or nae a Morishill". The house was largely rebuilt in 1842 for Alexander Shedden and by the 1870s was a residence of John Shedden Dobie, who published the enlargement of Pont's history of Cunninghame, which was begun by his father. More recent owners included John Watson, the Hope-Murray family, a Mr Butcher and finally a Mr Killner. It was demolished in 1970.

WAR MEMORIAL, BIGHOLM HILL, BEITH

On 6 November, 1920, Beith's War Memorial was unveiled on the Bigholm Hills near the Golf Club house. Robert McLachlan, a stonemason of Beith, had the sad task of carving the names on the memorial, including that of his own son, Pte Robert McLachlan of the Seaforth Highlands. In 1947 the memorial was moved to its current location at Janefield Place and a dedication service was held on 13 July that year, conducted by Rev. John Murray Woodburn with the praise being led by Beith Instrumental Band. An annual Remembrance Service, attended by the Royal British Legion and all uniform organisations in Beith as well as members of the public, continues to be held at the war memorial to honour local men who were killed in action.

Gateside is situated one mile east of Beith on the Lugton Road. It has a school, smiddy, inn, and a substantial village hall built in 1897 by the Ralston Patrick family of Trearne to commemorate their daughter Isabel who died at the early age of twenty-one. The village has a very active branch of the Women's Rural Institute which was formed in 1955 with a membership of thirty-six. Their motto is *Happiness all around only waiting to be found.* Gateside became the 47th Institute in Ayrshire and today has over eighty members. One of the most popular and highly respected villagers, local G.P. Dr John 'Johnny' Hibberd, died in March 2000 and the entire Beith and District community were very saddened at his passing. Johnny had been chairman of the Gateside Village Hall Committee for many years and a tireless worker for the village.

GATESIDE, BEITH.

Gateside has changed little except that the tenement properties have been largely replaced by modern houses. This view is taken from the western approach from Beith. The field on the left is a children's park and is used for the biannual village fete held to raise funds for the village hall. One prominent and greatly respected villager is the blacksmith, Robert Marshall, who still works in the smiddy to this day. The history of horse-shoeing at Gateside goes back more than a 125 years. John Marshall, Robert's grandfather, trained as a blacksmith in 1872 and in 1877 moved to Gateside, setting up the present smithy and living in the adjacent house. John died in 1911 after shoeing horses for thirty-four years, by which time he had a family of six daughters and three sons, Robert, William and the youngest, George. In the tradition of most businesses of the time, the youngest son carried on the trade. George was in business for fifty years until his death in 1961, at which time his youngest son, Robert, took over. The Marshalls held a centenary party in November 1977 to celebrate 100 years of their remarkable presence in Gateside and district.

This photograph of Barrmill was taken from the railway line leading to the Giffen Mill viaduct of the Caledonian line to Kilwinning via Giffen. The chimney in the immediate right of the picture was at the rear of Giffen Mill. The coal bing at the top right was located on ground to the rear of Balgray Road and the bridge carried a bogey line for delivering spoil to the tip. This coal pit was defunct by the late 1890s, although older Barrmill folk can recall sliding down the bing in happy childhood days. The bing was removed in the 1930s. The row to the left of the bing is known as Love's Building and still stands today. The large building (top and left of centre) is the Balgray Inn which was formerly known as the Trout Inn, Hillcrest Inn and Barrmill Inn. The extensive factory buildings on the left belonged to Crawford Brothers, thread manufacturers. William Harvey was the manager of the mill from the 1920s until its closure in 1946.

Crawford Brothers was established in 1775 at Crummock, Beith, but when the new mill was erected in 1836 at Barr Farm on the banks of the Dusk Water, the village of Barrmill expanded very quickly. The train which ran between Beith and Lugton and stopped at Barrmill was fondly known as 'the Johnny Beith' and it was very busy in the morning and evening with workers from the mill. In its heyday in the early 1900s, the mill employed 400 people and the thriving village had a Co-operative store, a reading and recreation room, a quoiting pitch, a railway station, two mission halls, a post office, and a pub. The two-storey buildings on the right housed some of the mill workers. These buildings no longer exist. The building left of centre is today used as a house, but was formerly the mill office. Crawford Brothers was later owned by Knox's of Kilbirnie and finally closed its doors in 1946.

The Braefoot Building was owned by Merry & Cunningham who controlled many local pits and coal mines in Ayrshire. The building, demolished in 1956, was situated on the north side of Beith Road in Barrmill. Many of the residents of the building then moved to council houses in Beith.

Beith Road, Barrmill.

Beith Road, Barrmill, looking east towards the centre of the village. All the buildings shown have been demolished and replaced with modern bungalows. When electric lighting was introduced to the village in 1933 Tom O'Kane wrote an eight verse poem appropriately entitled 'Barrmill's New Light': *For long it lay in darkness/ When winter nights were drear,/ But now it comes right up to date/ With lights that burn so clear./ All hail! Bright lights of Barrmill,/ You've wrought a wondrous charm,/ You show the way to one and all,/ And guide them from all harm.*

Greenhills · Barrmill

Greenhills village now consists of a few houses at the top of the Greenhills Brae. The building on the left was the former village school which served Barrmill, Burnhouse, the clachan of Hazelhead and the surrounding rural area. The school was later used as a glue factory and after the building was demolished a large private dwelling house was built on the site in the 1980s.

Burnhouse, Barrmill.

Burnhouse village, looking north towards Lugton. This road is now the very busy A736 between Irvine and Barrhead. In bygone times Burnhouse was known as 'The Trap' as there was an inn at the Barrmill/Dunlop crossroads further up the road where travellers, dealers and drovers gathered on route between Glasgow and the Ayrshire coast and were encouraged to linger and spend their money. The small place became so notorious that exasperated wives and mothers called the place 'The Man Trap', and eventually it became known simply as 'The Trap'.

THE OPEN-AIR LIFE AT BEITH.

Davies o' the Mill, located about a mile north of Beith, is the farm cottage in the foreground with Brimmer Farm in the background. This farm cottage was occupied by Dugald Semple from the early 1930s until around 1950. Semple was an outdoor enthusiast and ornithologist and he wrote a book entitled *A Free Man's Philosophy* in which he advocated the benefits of outdoor life. He kept a pony which pulled a gypsy type caravan seen on the right of the picture. Cyclists and walkers used to camp on ground at his cottage as illustrated in the photograph. He was regularly seen about Beith where he enjoyed talking to the townspeople and was known locally as 'The Bird Man'. A remarkable and fascinating character, he made regular trips to Ailsa Craig to study bird and plant life.

Little is known about Jock the Sweep other than that his name was John Gardiner and several distant relatives still reside in Beith today including John Irvine, aged 72. Jock was John's great-great-grandfather. The photograph dates from the 1880s when every house in Beith and surrounding villages would have had coal fires that required regular cleaning. Jock would have had a high degree of agility to traverse the roofs of the town with his poles and brushes and he was renowned for moving about roofs barefoot. People today will have little concept of coal fires and their sooty deposits, so this photograph is an interesting glimpse of an occupation which has all but disappeared. There were several other eccentric characters in Beith around this period including Dr Tish who dispensed medicine and advice; Wee Wull Tyler, who enjoyed a dram; Belle Bowstone, a washer woman; Heather Jock who sold heather and flowers; and a character who was strongly against religion and was known simply as 'Burn the Bible'.

FURTHER READING

Readers may find more information in the following books, some of which are available in the reference section of North Ayrshire Library Headquarters, Ardrossan. None of them are published by Stenlake Publishing.

The Statistical Account of Scotland, Vol. 6, Ayrshire, 1791–1799.
Michael C. Davis, *The Lost Mansions of Ayrshire,* 1984.
John Shedden Dobie (ed.), *Cunninghame Topographised by T. Pont 1604–1608,* 1876.
Moira Kinniburgh & Fiona Burke, *Kilbirnie & Glengarnock – Shared Memories,* 1995.
Sheila Pearson and the Gateside Hall Committee, *100 Years of Gateside Hall 1897–1997,* 1998.
Sam Porterfield, *Rambles Round Beith,* 1925.
Donald L. Reid, *The Beith Supplement – The Story of Beith's Newspaper,* 2000.
Donald L. Reid, *Reflections of Beith and District – On the Wings of Time,* 1994.
Donald L. Reid & Isobel F. Monahan (eds.), *Yesterday's Beith – A Pictorial Guide* 1999.
William Robertson, *Historic Ayrshire,* (1891)